Zebra

Deer

Siberian Tiger

Mountain Gorilla

Grizzly Bear

Beaver

European Wolf

Meerkat

Chipmunk

Hippopotamus

Wild Boar

Giant Panda

Prairie Dog

Hyena

Lynx

Lemur

Bison

Warthog

Camel

Red Deer

Possum

Polar Bear

Chimpanzee

Giant Tortoise

Published by
Peter Haddock Publishing,
United Kingdom YO16 6BT